# Our Colourful World

T0318092

## Contents

Written by Teresa Flavin

## Collins

# 1 Colour is all around

The world is alive with a rainbow of colours – red strawberries, orange tiger fur, yellow sunflowers, green forests, blue oceans, indigo birds, violet stones and much more.

Throughout history, people learnt how to turn nature's colours into dyes and **pigments**. This book explores the amazing ways that people coloured their artwork, clothing and even their food.

# 2 Rainbows of colour

Some of nature's most colourful features are rainbows. They appear in the sky when sunlight shines through raindrops. The light bends and **reflects** colours that make a rainbow.

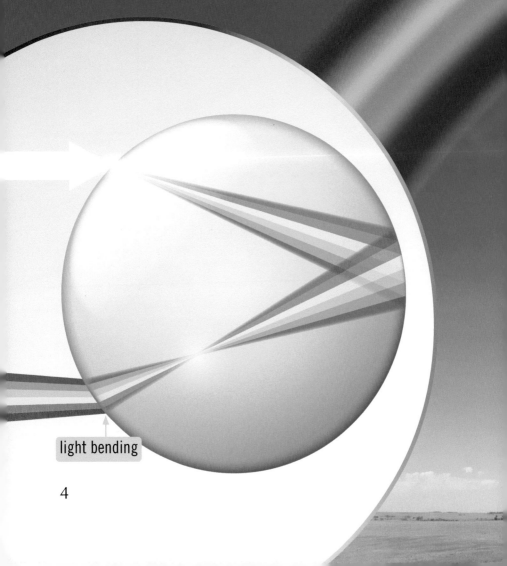

light bending

Today the rainbow is a symbol of hope and unity for many people.

Before people learnt how rainbows are formed, they told stories to explain where they came from. For example, some people believed rainbows were bridges to the sky.

# 3 What is colour?

Around 1665, the scientist Isaac Newton noticed how light splits into rainbow colours when it shines through a prism. He showed that colour comes from **wavelengths** of light. Each colour has its own wavelength.

Isaac Newton's prism experiment

Light wavelengths surround everything on Earth. When light touches a flower, some light is **absorbed** and some is reflected. The reflected light enters our eyes, which tell our brain what colour the flower is. In daytime, our eyes detect many colours reflected by light.

In the dark, we can see objects but we can't recognise their colours without reflected light.

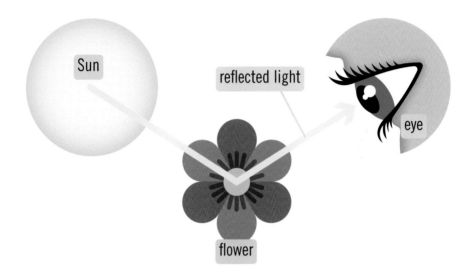

## Did you know?

When something absorbs all light wavelengths, it looks black. When something reflects all light wavelengths, it looks white.

# 4 Colour wheel

Colour wheels help artists to understand how colour works. Red, yellow and blue are called primary colours. Orange, green and violet are called secondary colours. Mixing two primary colours together makes a secondary colour.

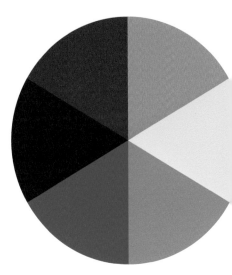

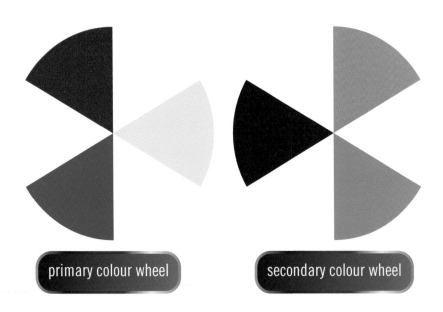

primary colour wheel

secondary colour wheel

Colours opposite each other on the wheel are called complementary colours. They look brighter next to each other.

## **Did you know?**

Look at the red apple for a few minutes, then look at the white space next to it. You may see a green apple, which is red's complementary colour.

9

# 5 Warm colours

Red, yellow and orange are called the warm colours. Some soil and rocks contain warm-coloured earth pigments called ochre. Ochre can be yellow, red or brown and is found all over the world. It has been used as a natural way of colouring and painting things for many thousands of years. Ancient cave paintings can still be seen today because ochre is so long-lasting.

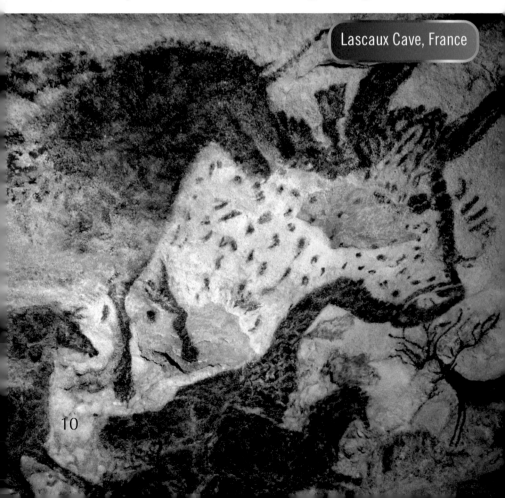

Lascaux Cave, France

Stone tools for grinding ochre and traces of pigment in **abalone** shells were discovered in Blombos Cave in South Africa. This shows that people made their own colours roughly 100,000 years ago.

a block of ochre and shells decorated with ochre, used as beads, found in Blombos Cave

## Did you know?

The Maasai people of East Africa paint red ochre on their faces and hair for important ceremonies.

# Red

Red is the colour of flowers and flames. From hearts to strawberries, red brings pleasure, but can also warn of danger. Red symbolises life because almost every living creature carries red blood inside it.

In China, red represents good fortune and is the most popular colour to wear and display during New Year.

In some Asian cultures, brides wear traditional red wedding dresses to bring good luck.

## Did you know?

The Aztec civilisation of Central America made red dye
from dried cochineal insects that live on prickly pear cacti.
Cochineal is used as a colour for cloth, foods and make-up.
It takes around 70,000 insects to make 500 grams of dye.
That's enough to fill one cereal or rice bowl.

13

# Yellow

Yellow is the colour of sunshine and warmth. From sunflowers to lemons, yellow brightens the world. The spices turmeric and saffron bring flavour to foods, and can be used to dye cloth yellow.

Saffron dye comes from threadlike parts inside a saffron crocus flower. Saffron is the most expensive spice in the world because so many flowers are needed, and they must be picked by hand.

JMW Turner was known to use gamboge in some of his watercolour paintings.

Artists once used a yellow paint named after the gamboge tree. People collected its **resin**, which hardened into brownish lumps. When a wet paintbrush touched the dried resin, it made a golden yellow pigment. But like some other yellow paints from long ago, gamboge often faded and was poisonous. Today's yellow paint colours are made using chemicals that are safer and more permanent.

# Orange

Orange is the colour of sunsets and autumn. From pumpkins to tigers, orange stands out. The word "orange" is believed to come from the sweet fruit that was probably first grown in China. A natural pigment called carotene gives many orange fruits, vegetables and flowers their colour.

## Did you know?

Carrots can be purple, white, red, yellow and orange. Hundreds of years ago, Dutch farmers produced the orange carrots known today.

In the 18th century, violins were sometimes varnished with a colour called dragon's blood that came from the dragon tree. This tree gives a resin that was mixed with oil to make the deep orange varnish.

dragon tree

dragon tree resin

An ancient myth told the story of dragon's blood. The story said that a dragon once hid in a tree and pounced on an elephant as it walked underneath. The battle was so fierce that their blood mixed together into the colour called dragon's blood.

an illustration of the myth of the dragon and elephant

# 6 Cool colours

Blue, green and violet are called the cool colours.
They remind people of water, sky, hills and forests.
Icebergs and **glaciers** look green, blue and violet because
of the way light reflects off them.

Artists often use cool colours to help warm colours stand out.
In the 19th century, artists such as Claude Monet and Vincent van Gogh put complementary colours together to make each colour look brighter.
Painting red next to green, blue next to orange, and violet next to yellow hadn't been done before. These artists showed that it worked well, and other artists started to experiment more with colour too.

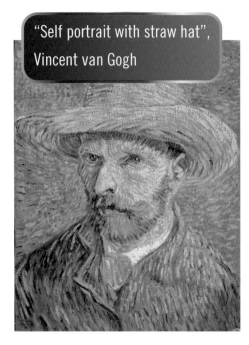

"Self portrait with straw hat", Vincent van Gogh

"Stacks of Wheat (End of Summer)", Claude Monet

19

# Blue

Blue is the colour of sky and ocean. From jeans to uniforms, people all over the world wear blue every day. Blue is often used to decorate stained glass, tiled walls and china teapots.

During the **Renaissance**, the best and most expensive blue pigment came from the lapis lazuli stone. In Europe, it was called ultramarine, which means "beyond the sea", because it was shipped over to Europe from Afghanistan.

"Girl with a Pearl Earring", Johannes Vermeer

lapis lazuli

The Mayan Mesoamerican civilisation of Central America believed that blue was sacred to their rain god Chac. They made blue pigment from the indigo plant mixed with mineral clay, and painted it onto objects to offer up to the rain god.

replica Mayan mural from Bonampak in Chiapas, Mexico

indigo plant

# Green

Green is the colour of gardens and forests. From green frogs and snakes to parrots and fish, green is **abundant** in nature.

To ancient Egyptians, green represented growth and **vegetation**. Osiris, their god of the underworld, was shown with a green face symbolising rebirth. The Egyptians made one of the first green paints from a rock called malachite. They even used green makeup because they thought it would protect them from evil.

malachite stone

Osiris

A chemist named Scheele created a green dye that was used on many wallpapers and fabrics in the 19th century. But people fell ill from Scheele's green because it contained a dangerous chemical called arsenic. New, safer ways of making green dye were found.

Scheele's green wallpaper

## Did you know?

Today, green is used to show something is environmentally friendly.

# Violet

Violet is the colour of blossoms and fruits.

In the ancient lands around the Mediterranean Sea, only royalty and emperors could wear a colour called Tyrian purple because it was more expensive than gold. This purple dye came from the murex snail's **mucus**. Each snail could only give a drop once. It took over 10,000 snails to make enough dye to colour the trim of one cloak. Like red made from cochineal insects and yellow made from saffron flowers, Tyrian purple was one of the most valuable natural dyes ever, until others replaced it.

Empress Theodora, from the 6th century, wearing Tyrian purple

murex snail shells

William Perkin

In 1856 William Perkin, a young Chemistry student, tried to find a cure for **malaria** using a liquid that came from coal. Instead, his chemical experiments created a permanent purple dye that became known as "mauve" after a purple flower. Perkin's method of making mauve led to the production of many other permanent dye colours made today.

### Did you know?

Queen Victoria started a fashion for dresses in the new mauve colour.

25

# 7 Colourful you

When you see a rainbow, remember how light makes those colours and how your eyes see them. Thanks to people from the past who experimented with the dyes and pigments found in nature, today's colours are more permanent and varied than ever. People can choose their clothes and belongings in any shade from a dazzling rainbow of colours.

# Glossary

**abalone** shellfish with mother-of-pearl inside its shell

**absorbed** took something in

**abundant** plentiful

**glaciers** large masses of ice

**Iron Age** a time in early history when people learned how to make iron tools and weapons

**malaria** disease spread by mosquitoes

**mucus** thick liquid made inside a body

**pigments** substances that give something a particular colour

**reflects** bounces light off a surface

**Renaissance** a time in Europe in the 14th, 15th and 16th centuries when a lot of new ideas in science, literature and art were explored

**resin** thick liquid inside a plant

**vegetation** plants, trees and flowers

**wavelength** distance between two waves of energy

# Index

# A world of colour

cochineal insects

ochre

saffron crocus flowers

gamboge resin

lapis lazuli stone

indigo plant

  malachite stone  nature (gardens/green frogs)

  natural carotene pigment  dragon's blood resin

  snail mucus  liquid from coal

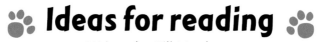

# Ideas for reading

Written by Gill Matthews
*Primary Literacy Consultant*

**Reading objectives:**
- identify main ideas drawn from more than one paragraph and summarise these
- identify how language, structure, and presentation contribute to meaning
- retrieve and record information from non-fiction

**Spoken language objectives:**
- articulate and justify answers, arguments and opinions
- use spoken language to develop understanding through speculating, hypothesising, imagining and exploring ideas

**Curriculum links:** Science – Light; Art

**Interest words:** primary, secondary, complementary

**Resources:** paint, brushes, pots, paper, collage materials; IT

## Build a context for reading

- Ask children to read the front and back covers of the book and to suggest what they might find out from reading it.
- Challenge them to note down as many colours as they can in two minutes. Take feedback and identify which colour was noted down the most and which the least.
- Ask what features they expect the book to have. Give them time to skim the book and to find the contents, glossary and index. Discuss the purpose and organisation of each feature.

## Understand and apply reading strategies

- Ask children to use the contents to find the chapter called "Colour is all around". Read pp2–3 aloud. Discuss why the word *pigments* is in bold. Give children time to look up the word in the glossary.
- Read pp4–5 and discuss children's experiences of rainbows. Model how to summarise the information on pp2–5 by identifying the main points in each paragraph.
- Ask children to read Chapters 3 and 4 and to note down a summary of the information. Take feedback. Challenge them to do the "Did you know?" activity on page 9.